A Little
of God's Wisdom & Wit
for Women

Written and Compiled by
Kathleen Richards & Varsi Atkinson

Victory House, Inc.
Tulsa, Oklahoma

A LITTLE BIT OF GOD'S WISDOM AND WIT FOR WOMEN

Published by Victory House, Inc.
P.O. Box 700238
Tulsa, Oklahoma 74170
(918) 747-5009

Cover Design by: *Whitley Graphics*
Cover Illustration by: *Dawne Erickson*

INTRODUCTION

The author of the Book of Proverbs writes, "How good is a timely word!" (Prov. 15:23, NIV). Women from all walks of life who use this book have echoed his exclamation as they have discovered new insights for living in the timely words and sagely advice presented here.

This is a gentle book for the woman of the nineties who wants to experience all life has to offer. Indeed, it is for every woman — young or old, single or married. Prepared by women for women, this little book speaks to our hearts in ways that remind us not to take ourselves too seriously, to be gentle with ourselves, and to quiet our minds in this busy world.

A Little Bit of God's Wisdom and Wit for Women is for you to cherish and enjoy. As you meditate upon its timely words, you will be refreshed, and you will see everything from a new perspective.

To Our Readers

If you have favorite humorous or wise sayings or anecdotes that we could include in future books, please send them to:

Kathleen Richards & Varsi Atkinson
c/o Victory House, Inc.
P.O. Box 700238
Tulsa, OK 74170

Books of Interest

A Little Bit of God's Wisdom and Wit
A Little Bit of God's Wisdom and Wit for Men
A Little Bit of God's Wisdom and Wit for Women
Prayers That Prevail — The Believer's Manual of Prayers
Prayers That Prevail for America — Changing a Nation Through Prayer
Prayers That Prevail for Your Children — A Parent's and Grandparent's
　Manual of Prayers

All titles are available at your local
bookstore or through Victory House, Inc.

According to God, only two things are worth more than rubies — wisdom and a virtuous woman.

❦

A virtuous woman....her price is far above rubies.
(Proverbs 31:10)

Earth's noblest thing, a woman perfected.

(James Russell Lowell)

You are complete in Him.
(Colossians 2:10, NKJV).

Beauty is not caused. It is.

(Emily Dickinson)

Behold, you are fair, my love! Behold, you are fair!
(Song of Solomon 1:15, NKJV)

Any wife with an inferiority complex can cure it by being sick in bed for a day while her husband manages the household and the children.

(Eleanor Field)

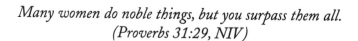

Many women do noble things, but you surpass them all.
(Proverbs 31:29, NIV)

For balance in life, it is wise to have both a dog that adores you and a cat that ignores you.

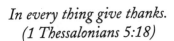

In every thing give thanks.
(1 Thessalonians 5:18)

Patience makes a woman beautiful in middle age.

(Elliot Paul)

Let patience have her perfect work.
(James 1:4)

It's impossible for a woman to be married to the same man for fifty years. After the first twenty-five, he's not the same man.

(Jim Garis)

But a woman who fears the Lord, she shall be praised.
(Proverbs 31:30, NKJV).

Women and elephants never forget.

(Dorothy Parker)

Old age is when you know all the answers but nobody asks you the questions.

(Anonymous)

The heart that loves is always young.

Let us consider one another in order to stir up love and good works.
(Hebrews 10:24, NKJV)

Your responsibility is your response to His ability.

I can do all things through Christ who strengthens me.
(Philippians 4:13, NKJV)

You may search my time-worn face. You'll find a merry eye that twinkles. I am not an old lady, just a little girl with wrinkles!

Edythe E. Bregnard

The hardest years in life are those between ten and seventy.

Helen Hayes

Charm is a glow within a woman which casts a most becoming light on others.

(John Mason Brown)

In all things showing yourself to be a pattern of good works.
(Titus 2:7, NKJV)

You can give without loving, but you cannot love without giving.

For God so loved the world, that he gave....
(John 3:16)

Insanity is hereditary. You can get it from your children.

(Sam Levenson)

If teenagers want to be so different, why do they dress alike?

As you shut the door to your past, walk into newness of life.

We also should walk in newness of life.
(Romans 6:4)

You cannot uproot a life that is rooted in God.

And he shall be like a tree planted by the rivers of water.
(Psalms 1:3)

Remember, Ginger Rogers did everything Fred Astaire did, but she did it backwards and in high heels.

(Faith Whittlesey)

When I was born, I was so surprised I couldn't talk for a year and a half.

(Gracie Allen)

One today is worth two tomorrows.

(Benjamin Franklin)

This is the day the Lord has made; let us rejoice and be glad in it.
(Psalm 118:24, NIV)

I am not afraid of tomorrow, for I have seen yesterday and I love today.

(William Allen White)

Therefore do not worry about tomorrow, for tomorrow will worry about its own things.
(Matthew 6:34, NKJV)

Prayer is asking for rain. Faith is carrying the umbrella.

The wings of prayer soar high and far.

For your Father knows the things you have need of before you ask Him.
(Matthew 6:8, NKJV)

Careful for nothing, prayerful for everything, thankful for anything.

(Dwight L. Moody)

*In everything give thanks; for this is the will of God
in Christ Jesus for you.
(1 Thessalonians 5:18, NKJV)*

God will either give you what you ask, or something far better.

(Robert M. McCheyne)

All things work together for good to them that love God.
(Romans 8:28)

When God measures a person, He puts the tape around the heart, not around the head.

O God, my heart is fixed.
(Psalms 108:1)

God knows your load limit, and He will limit your load.

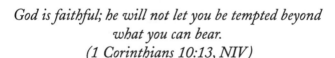

*God is faithful; he will not let you be tempted beyond
what you can bear.
(1 Corinthians 10:13, NIV)*

Laugh and the world laughs with you — cry and you streak your mascara.

(Anonymous)

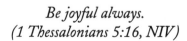

Be joyful always.
(1 Thessalonians 5:16, NIV)

Laughter is the brush that sweeps away the cobwebs of the heart.

(Mort Walker)

With God we will gain the victory.
(Psalm 108:13, NIV)

I pray hard, work hard and leave the rest to God.

(Florence Griffith Joyner)

You're as happy as you allow yourself to be. So, why be unhappy?

(Marilyn Quayle)

The best proof of love is trust.

(Joyce Brothers)

You are all sons of light and sons of the day.
(1 Thessalonians 5:5, NKJV)

Love seeks to make happy as well as to be happy.

Love covers over a multitude of sins.
(1 Peter 4:8, NIV)

No one can make you feel inferior without your consent.

(Eleanor Roosevelt)

But we have this treasure in earthen vessels, that the excellency of the power may be of God, and not of us.
(2 Corinthians 4:7)

I'm special. In all the world there's nobody like me.

(Anonymous)

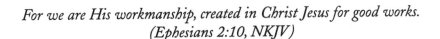

For we are His workmanship, created in Christ Jesus for good works.
(Ephesians 2:10, NKJV)

The persons hardest to convince they're at the retirement age are children at bedtime.

(Shannon Fife)

Children, obey your parents in the Lord, for this is right.
(Ephesians 6:1, NIV)

It's nice for children to have pets until the pets start having children.

Let the peace of God rule in your hearts.
(Colossians 3:15)

Few things are more satisfying than seeing your children have teenagers of their own.

(Doug Larson)

Ask your child what he wants for dinner only if he's buying.

(Fran Lebowitz)

A merry heart does good like medicine.
(Proverbs 17:22, NKJV)

If a door slams shut look for the one God is opening for you.

*For I know the plans I have for you, declares the Lord.
(Jeremiah 29:11, NIV)*

The sign on the door of opportunity says, "Push."

I press toward the mark for the prize of the high calling of God in Christ Jesus.
(Philippians 3:14)

A vacation is having nothing to do and all day to do it in.

(Robert Orben)

I will greatly praise the Lord with my mouth.
(Psalms 109:30)

The will of God will never lead you where the grace of God cannot keep you.

My grace is sufficient for thee.
(2 Corinthians 12:9)

Those who don't know how to weep with their whole heart, don't know how to laugh either.

(Golda Meir)

We can do no great things - only small things with great love.

(Mother Teresa)

A wise woman said, "If you want the rainbow, you have to put up with some rain."

*He makes His sun to rise on the evil and on the good,
and sends rain on the just and on the unjust.
(Matthew 5:45)*

Well done is better than well said.

(Benjamin Franklin)

Therefore by their fruits you will know them.
(Matthew 7:20, NKJV)

Happiness is not a goal, it is a by-product.

(Eleanor Roosevelt)

If you really want to be happy, nobody can stop you.

(Sister Mary Trickey)

You are the apple of God's eye.

Keep me as the apple of the eye, hide me under the shadow of thy wings.
(Psalms 17:8)

Don't bother to give God instructions; just report for duty.

(Corrie ten Boom)

To have a friend, be a friend.

A friend loves at all times, and a brother is born for adversity.
(Proverbs 17:17, NKJV)

A true friend is one who knows all about you, and likes you just the same.

A happy heart is better than a full purse.

(Italian proverb)

But he who is of a merry heart has a continual feast.
(Proverbs 15:15, NKJV)

A thankful heart is the parent of all virtues.

(Cicero)

In every thing give thanks.
(1 Thessalonians 5:18)

Do your best, and trust God to do the rest.

Without Me you can do nothing.
(John 15:5, NKJV)

Faith does to a life what sunshine does to stained glass.

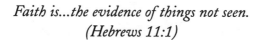

Faith is...the evidence of things not seen.
(Hebrews 11:1)

Love is the condition in which the happiness of another person is essential to your own.

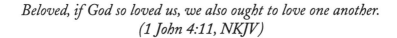

Beloved, if God so loved us, we also ought to love one another.
(1 John 4:11, NKJV)

Love, you know, seeks to make happy rather than to be happy.

(Ralph Connor)

A new commandment I give to you, that you love one another.
(John 13:34, NKJV)

Faith is believing what you do not yet see: its reward is to see what you believe.

(Augustine)

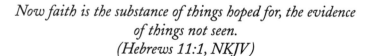

*Now faith is the substance of things hoped for, the evidence
of things not seen.
(Hebrews 11:1, NKJV)*

Faith is the mouth which feeds on Christ.

(Charles Haddon Spurgeon)

The word is near you, even in your mouth and in your heart.
(Romans 10:8, NKJV)

Everyone else my age is an adult, whereas I am merely in disguise.

(Margaret Atwood)

Age seldom arrives smoothly or quickly. It's more often a succession of jerks.

(Jean Rhys)

All we really need, we have in Jesus.

(Susan M. Bailey)

I can do all things through Christ who strengthens me.
(Philippians 4:13, NKJV)

We come closest to God at our lowest moments.

(Terry Anderson)

Be strong in the Lord, and in the power of his might.
(Ephesians 6:10)

Let me take time for beauty, Lord.

(Marjorie Holmes)

Come aside by yourselves to a deserted place and rest a while.
(Mark 6:31, NKJV)

As for butter versus margarine, I trust cows more than chemists.

(Joan Gussow)

Fear knocked at the door.
Faith answered.
No one was there.

(Inscription at Hind's Head Inn in England)

Be not afraid, only believe.
(Mark 5:36)

A genuine faith sings songs in the darkest night.

And call upon me in the day of trouble: I will deliver thee,
and thou shalt glorify me.
(Psalms 50:15)

Hold your child's hand while he or she will let you.

Children are an heritage of the Lord.
(Psalms 127:3)

Children are the hands by which we take hold of heaven.

(Henry Ward Beecher)

Always forgive your enemies; nothing annoys them so much.

(Oscar Wilde)

Love your enemies....
(Matthew 5:44)

It is by forgiving that one is forgiven.

(Mother Teresa)

Inside every seventy-year-old is a thirty-five-year-old asking: "What happened?"

(Ann Landers)

Therefore we do not lose heart. Though outwardly we are wasting away, yet inwardly we are being renewed day by day.
(2 Corinthians 4:16, NIV)

Do not deprive me of my age. I have earned it.

(May Sarton)

Every believer is God's miracle.

(Philip James Bailey)

Many believed in his name, when they saw the miracles which he did.
(John 2:23)

Expect a miracle.

He was exceeding glad....and he hoped to have seen
some miracle done by Him.
(Luke 23:8)

In His will is our peace.

(Dante)

To be spiritually minded is life and peace.
(Romans 8:6)

The secret of true strength is found in a peaceful mind.

The peace of God, which passeth all understanding, shall keep your hearts and minds through Christ Jesus.
(Philippians 4:7)

Faith is knowing there is an ocean because you have seen a brook.

(William Arthur Ward)

*Now faith is the substance of things hoped for,
the evidence of things not seen.
(Hebrews 11:1)*

Faith is a refusal to panic.

(D. Martyn Lloyd-Jones)

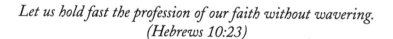

Let us hold fast the profession of our faith without wavering.
(Hebrews 10:23)

I can keep a secret, but the folks I tell it to can't.

To keep your secret is wisdom; but to expect others to keep it is folly.

(Samuel Johnson)

Better is the poor who walks in his integrity, than one who is perverse in his lips, and is a fool.
(Proverbs 19:1, NKJV)

If the people around you are uncomfortable with your singing, change pews.

Make a joyful noise unto God.
(Psalms 66:1)

Joy is the holy fire that keeps our purpose warm and our intelligence aglow.

(Helen Keller)

The joy of the Lord is your strength.
(Nehemiah 8:10)

God is there every morning.

The Lord's mercies...are new every morning. Great is your faithfulness.
(Lamentations 3:23, 24, NKJV)

This day is God's.

This is the day which the Lord hath made;
we will rejoice and be glad in it.
(Psalms 118:24)

If life is a bowl of cherries, what am I doing in the pits?

(Erma Bombeck)

There is no pit so deep that Jesus is not deeper still.

(Corrie ten Boom)

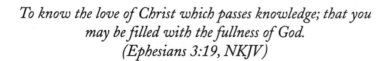

To know the love of Christ which passes knowledge; that you may be filled with the fullness of God.
(Ephesians 3:19, NKJV)

Strangers are friends that you have yet to meet.

(Roberta Lieberman)

A man who has friends must himself be friendly.
(Proverbs 18:24, NKJV)

You cannot use your friends and have them too.

A friend loves at all times, and a brother is born for adversity.
(Proverbs 17:17, NKJV)

It is better to knit than to needle.

She selects wool and flax and works with eager hands.
(Proverbs 31:13, NIV)

When you have nothing to say, say nothing.

He who guards his mouth preserves his life.
(Proverbs 13:3, NKJV)

A good laugh is sunshine in a house.

(Thackeray)

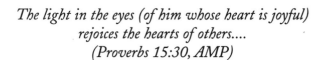

*The light in the eyes (of him whose heart is joyful)
rejoices the hearts of others....
(Proverbs 15:30, AMP)*

Happiness is a choice. Reach out for it at the time it appears.

(Adair Lara)

Rejoice, and be exceeding glad.
(Matthew 5:12)

When it comes to giving think not what can I spare; think, what can I share?

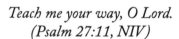

Teach me your way, O Lord.
(Psalm 27:11, NIV)

God loves cheerful givers, but He will accept the offering of a grouch as well.

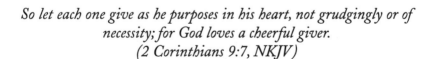

So let each one give as he purposes in his heart, not grudgingly or of necessity; for God loves a cheerful giver.
(2 Corinthians 9:7, NKJV)

Tea, to the English, is really a picnic indoors.

(Alice Walker)

When you are on your knees you cannot stumble.

They shall call on my name, and I will hear them.
(Zechariah 13:9, NKJV)

People who fly into a rage always make a bad landing.

(Will Rogers)

For the wrath of man does not produce the righteousness of God.
(James 1:20, NKJV)

I am born happy every morning.

(Edith Wharton)

This is the day the Lord has made; let us rejoice and be glad in it.
(Psalm 118:24, NIV)

God is not finished with you.

For we are His workmanship, created in Christ Jesus for good works,
which God prepared beforehand that we should walk in them.
(Ephesians 2:10, NKJV)

You can never praise God too much.

O magnify the Lord with me, and let us exalt his name together.
(Psalms 34:3)

A woman is like a tea bag. You never know how strong she is until she gets into hot water.

(Eleanor Roosevelt)

As one goes through life one learns that if you don't paddle your own canoe, you don't move.

(Katharine Hepburn)

Religion is easier caught, than taught.

Peacemakers who sow in peace raise a harvest of righteousness.
(James 3:18, NIV)

Make good choices today.

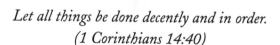

Let all things be done decently and in order.
(1 Corinthians 14:40)

What used to be old is middle-aged now, and what used to be ancient is just old.

(Joyce Brothers)

Old age is like a plane flying through a storm. Once you're aboard, there's nothing you can do.

(Golda Meir)

To love is to admire with the heart; to admire is to love with the mind.

(Theophile Gautier)

We love Him because He first loved us.
.(1 John 4:19, NKJV)

What sunshine is to flowers, smiles are to humanity.

(Joseph Addison)

Beloved, if God so loved us, we also ought to love one another.
(1 John 4:11, NKJV)

The more time you invest in a marriage, the more valuable it becomes.

(Amy Grant)

Marriage is an investment that pays you dividends if you pay interest.

(Anonymous)

*Then they can train the younger women to love
their husbands and children.*
(Titus 2:4, NIV)

A faithful friend is a strong defense; and he that hath found him hath found a treasure.

(Louisa May Alcott)

I am wealthy in my friends.

(William Shakespeare)

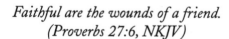

Faithful are the wounds of a friend.
(Proverbs 27:6, NKJV)

Have you noticed when you run out of places to turn, He's always there?

I am with you always, even to the end of the age.
(Matthew 28:20, NKJV)

You are never alone.

I will never leave you nor forsake you.
(Hebrews 13:5, NKJV)

God's love does not always keep us from trials, but it is a love that always keeps us through trials.

Never be afraid to trust an unknown future to a known God.

The way to love anything is to realize that it might be lost.

(G.K. Chesterton)

Let love be without hypocrisy.
(Romans 12:9, NKJV)

To love is to
comparir

(Bernard Grasset)

Beloved, if God so loved us, we ought also to love one another.
(1 John 4:11)

We could never learn to be brave and patient, if there were only joy in the world.

(Helen Keller)

Joy runs deeper than despair.

(Corrie ten Boom)

Some things come out
better without our
help...like a bud opening
into a beautiful flower.

Are you a blossom on your family tree?

Rejoice in the Lord always. Again I will say rejoice!
(Philippians 4:4, NKJV)

Before you go to bed, turn your worries over to God. He'll be up all night.

He who watches over you will not slumber.
(Psalm 121:3, NIV)

I never take a problem to bed with me at night.

(Harry S. Truman)

Casting all your care upon Him, for He cares for you.
(1 Peter 5:7, NKJV)

Nothing is more frequently "opened by mistake" than the mouth.

It is easier to recover from a slip of the foot than a slip of the tongue.

Keep your tongue from evil and your lips from speaking lies.
(Psalm 34:13, NIV)

Focus on the promises of God instead of the problems of life.

For all the promises of God in Him are Yes, and in Him Amen,
to the glory of God through us.
(2 Corinthians 1:20, NKJV)

His [God's] promise is a threefold cord that cannot be broken.

(Andrew Murray)

If you believe, you will receive whatever you ask for in prayer.
(Matthew 21:22, NIV)

The future belongs to those who believe in the beauty of their dreams.

(Eleanor Roosevelt)

Where there is no vision, the people perish.
(Proverbs 29:18)

The more you are thankful for what you have, the more you will have to be thankful for.

(Zig Ziglar)

Never insult an alligator until after you have crossed the river.

(Cordell Hull)

Let your gentleness be known to all men.
(Philippians 4:5, NKJV)

A hammer sometimes misses its mark — a bouquet never.

(Monta Crane)

Each of you should look not only to your own interests,
but also to the interests of others.
(Philippians 2:4, NIV)

You see much more of your children once they leave home.

(Lucille Ball)

I'm going to stop punishing my children by saying, "Never mind! I'll do it myself."

(Erma Bombeck)

A short memory is a very useful thing.

For if you forgive men when they sin against you,
your heavenly Father will also forgive you.
(Matthew 6:14, NIV)

Being an adult is dirty work, but someone has to do it.

(Robert Fulghum)

I will praise You, O Lord my God, with all my heart,
And I will glorify Your name forevermore.
(Psalm 86:12, NKJV)

There is no cosmetic for beauty like happiness.

(Lady Marguerite Blessington)

A merry heart makes a cheerful countenance, But by sorrow of the heart the spirit is broken.
(Proverbs 15:13, NKJV)

Cheerfulness, like spring, opens all the blossoms of the inward man.

(Jean Paul Richter)

Be of good cheer.
(Matthew 9:2)

The ideal woman for me is one with whom I can cry.

(Enzo Biagi)

*Carry each other's burdens, and in this way
you will fulfill the law of Christ.
(Galatians 6:2, NIV)*

You may forget with whom you laughed, but you will never forget with whom you wept.

Rejoice with them that do rejoice, and weep with them that weep.
(Romans 12:15)

"Stay" is a charming word in a friend's vocabulary.

(Louisa May Alcott)

On the road between the homes of friends, grass does not grow.

(Norwegian proverb)

The sunshine of God's love brightens every day.

This is love, that we walk according to His commandments.
(2 John 6, NKJV)

Happiness comes from within.

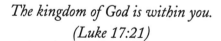

The kingdom of God is within you.
(Luke 17:21)

The way to see by faith is to shut the eye of reason.

(Benjamin Franklin)

Trust in the Lord with all your heart, and lean not on your own understanding.
(Proverbs 3:5, NKJV)

Believing is seeing.

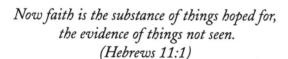

Now faith is the substance of things hoped for,
the evidence of things not seen.
(Hebrews 11:1)

Patience is a virtue that carries a lot of wait.

Wait on the Lord: be of good courage, and He shall strengthen your heart: wait, I say, on the Lord.
(Psalm 27:14, NKJV)

We can do anything we want to do if we stick to it long enough.

(Helen Keller)

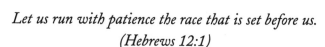

Let us run with patience the race that is set before us.
(Hebrews 12:1)

I'm going to clean this dump — just as soon as the kids are grown.

(Erma Bombeck)

This day is a gift; that's why we call it the present.

Rejoice evermore.
(1 Thessalonians 5:16, NKJV)

Jesus chose you!

You did not choose Me, but I chose you and appointed you that you should go and bear fruit.
(John 15:16, NKJV)